Speaking Pictures

a collection of poems and lyric verse
to encourage a looking beyond
those things which are seen

Alfred C. Gerrity

© Copyright Alfred Gerrity 2023

This book is sold subject to the conditions: it is not, by way of trade or otherwise, lent, hired out, or otherwise circulated in any form of binding or cover other than that in which it is published . No part of this publication may be reproduced, stored in a retrieval system, or transmitted in any form or by any means (electronic, mechanical, photocopying, recording, or otherwise) without prior written permission from the Publisher

FIRST EDITION

ISBN: 978-1-7391921-8-1 Paperback

"Speaking Pictures: A collection of poems and lyric verse to

encourage a looking beyond those things which are seen" by Alfred C. Gerrity

For more information, please direct your emails to:
info@ibelieveican.co.uk

Bible scripture taken from NKJV

TC PUBLISHING

Contents

For my daughter Andrea

English

Psalm 107:43

Whoever is wise will observe these things, and they will understand the lovingkindness of the Lord.

French

Psaume 107:43

Que celui qui est sage prenne garde à ces choses,
Et qu'il soit attentif aux bontés de l'Éternel.

German

Psalm 107:43

Wer klug ist,achtet darauf und wird erkennen,
wie viel Wohltaten der Herr erzeigt.

Spanish

Salmo 107:43

Quien sea sabio,que considere estas cosas,
Y entienda a bien el gran amor del Senor

A Riddle

(for Andrea)

I bring a message from far away,
for you, just you, for you today.

Whenever I'm asked to do such as this,
I take special aim and never miss.

I'm old like the wind and young as the day,
and I`ll always have time to come your way.

I'm gentle as a whisper and strong as a man,
so tell me, do you know who I am?

J`apporte un message de loin

Pour vous, juste vous, pour vous ce jour

Memories of Rhugarbh

(for Andrea and Steve)

I know a place where there are pegs on the line. A place
in the north where dwells a daughter of mine.

She goes out to hang her washing, in the space between
the house and the barn, a space that for us seems to
possess a strange and lovely charm.

The barn now is the domain of a practical man, where
once the owl did rule and his hunting would plan.

Standing there also was an old-fashioned wardrobe,
empty and still, bereft now of clothes, and thus its
purpose to fulfil.

Before the breaking up, we took some coat hooks
and a handle the colour of amber, so at least we have
something of its former grandeur to remember.

In memory then we fondly recall those early days,
mostly of that special little one, who simply by his
presence, made all things for us at Rhugarbh complete.

While in the here and now, we welcome another friend, who by her gentle company will ensure that such blessings will come again and repeat.

So then, in all these things and more, we see Providence bright shining like a star, arranging and guiding, and doing all things to bring us safe thus far.

On A Winter's Morning

(for Andrea and Steve)

On a winter's morning, the three of us went for a walk along the beach – our silent footprints in the sand, giving a momentary substance to each.

Then we clambered over the rocks, at times slipping and sliding, till we saw that our way was cut off, by sea and tide now rising.

So up a rusty ladder we climbed, each of us turning to give a hand to the one behind –and there in that good time of simply being sociable, we saw the great truth, hidden in the Master's parable.

Remembrance

(for Andrea)

How she reminded me of you, there in that gentle
distance between the one and two.

She had come from across the way, as if drawn by
firelight to this man working on a winter's day.

How I laughed when she said 'she was eight but turning
into nine.' Then how marvellous I thought, to share so
much in so little time.

As I turned away to paint the door she said "Go on then,
ask me another sum just like before."- "Okay." I said,
"But this must be the last." Pushing hard December light
now fading fast "What is twenty times ten?"

Taking a breath to do her best, she closed her eyes – as if to see more clearly, the shape and size of this final test.

Christmas eve, a painter and a brush and all time it seemed – waited – hushed.

How good to be reminded of you, there in that gentle distance between the one and two.

The Fledgeling

(for Andrea)

Here on the ridge, I am nearer to the sky,
but now I cannot fly.

New horizons all around I see, yet they remain still too distant for me.

I watch and see how with so much joy - the others fly.

Swooping and gliding - higher and high.

Now, with my mouth I am learning how to call - and of the three of us, I was the first to stand tall.

Day by day I groom and grow, waiting for the time that only I will know.

Who then - is the One who made us like this? So that we on wings should know such bliss.

Two Ways

Come listen while I share with you – things we ought to know.

About words that were spoken and heard so long ago.

They tell us about the two ways that everyone will go.

There are two ways before us, the high way and the low.

So, turn around and take a look now, you see the high and the low.

Turn around and take a look now – and choose the way you will go.

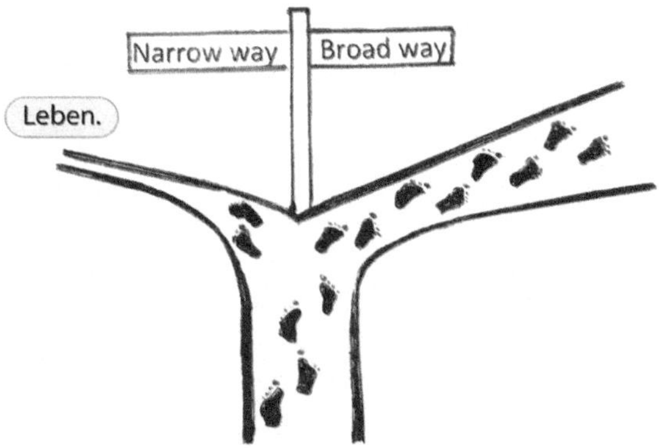

Die Zwei Wege, die jeder gehen wird.

Beneficence

(for Andrea)

How generous are the trees who bear their fruit for us to please.

How willing are the plants to grow, yet how these wonders work, do we really know?

Then there is the sun, rain and soil. The lovely lilies of the field, who do not need to labour or toil.

Neither does this kindness come but once and then an end. Nor does this common grace on any goodness of ours depend.

We watch the seasons as they turn, seeing how all these things come again and return. So then, is there a message in all this to tell? Surely yes! for it's as clear as a bell.

Who Is This?

(for Steve and Andrea)

What did it mean, that break in the clouds on such a dark and gloomy day?

The flash of light and streak of sunlight, that lit up our way.

She said it was a sign –was it really something meant to encourage and help us hold the line?

But what if some do not believe in the One Most High –would that, such a gracious message nullify?

Others have been like watchmen on the wall, awake, having light, yet looking beyond to the one who has the answer to it all.

Who is this? The Alpha and the Omega, the First and the Last, the Beginning and the End. Who is this?

The Paper Christmas Tree

(for Andrea)

I am just a paper Christmas tree that fell among the feet.

Who knows the hand that fashioned me so vulnerable, so sweet?

I am just a light in the darkness, a very basic thing.

My only strength is gentleness and of me, the carols sing.

I am just the hand that holds you, my precious bauble in space.

Surely now you know me, now you have seen my face.

Ma précieux boule dans l'espace

Music

(for Keith Mathews
and our Maria)

“Why do you come with your music?” they say. “What good will it do anyway?”

But we were there together at Christmas,
to watch and hear them sing and play.

We saw that music, like some great universal smile. Does not need to reason why, nor will one ever need to justify.

How Sweet Life Is

(for our Dot)

How sweet life is, when the sun is on your face. With your eyes closed and a smile on your lips. Because you know that God is good.

How sweet life is, now that you are well again, With hope and a future and praise on your lips. Because you know that God is good.

Fear had come like a thief in the night. To steal your peace away. But mercy was right by your side and grace came with the day.

So be at rest in your soul once more, and always remember, never forget, how the Lord has been good to you.

A Message For The Young

(for Andrea and Steve)

Did they never, ever tell you, just how wonderful you
are? There is no one like you under the sun, you're the
most amazing by far, oh yes, you are.

But where on earth did you come from? Did you come
from the sea?
But you can sing like an angel, so that cannot be.

But where on earth did you come from? Did you
fall from the sky? You must have dropped down by
parachute, for only eagles can fly, fly that high.

Did you ever, ever wonder, what they have been telling
you? They seem so sure they have the answer, but is it
really true? What they have been telling you?

You did not come like an astronaut, from a distant galaxy. You did not come like a creeping thing, crawling out of the sea.
No, no, you did not come from the sea.

You were made by a loving hand, by a royal decree. You were given the image of a king, we cannot see now, but one day we will see. Oh yes, one day we will see,

Now I know where you came from. There really is no mystery. I did not look in a science book. I did not go to the local library.

I just go and lift up my eyes to the heavens above. I hear them telling us the true story – it is a story of love – Oh yes – it is a story of love.

I Love What You Love

(for our Jane)

Whenever I think of you, I feel good.

Whenever I have been with you, I feel better.

Why should this be?

To us there is no mystery - it's just love going back and forth. Like a ball played with grace.

"Anyone for love?" I hear you say, our gentle Jane.

Yes! I will play - for I love what you love - and you love what is lovely.

"Tenez! – êtes-vous prêt à recevoir?"

Trust

Forbid it Lord that I turn from you and find my comfort in something new.

Always at your side, I will be, delighting in your company.

Yes, Lord, I do trust in you and acknowledge you in all I do.

Yes, Lord, you're my guiding light, for who but our God does shine so bright.

Forget not yet all His kindness, His common grace for us all to bless.

And let not your heart be hardened but turn and seek your pardon.

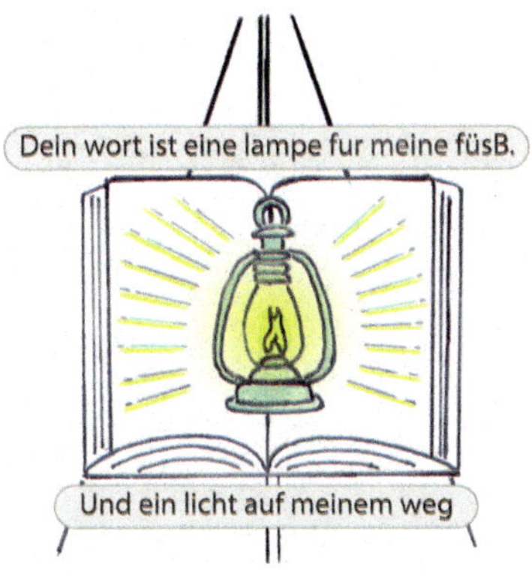

Wisdom

How sweet does wisdom seem to me, sweeter than honey from the comb.

More precious than rubies, her path will lead us home - will lead us home.

She cries out in every busy street - she raises her voice wherever people meet.

Come! bring your simple ones to me.

So, men and maidens everywhere, all you who are living for today. Seek you after Wisdom and she will guide your way - and keep you safe until that day.

Immanuel (God is with us)

(for Andrea and Steve)

We have a wonderful tale to tell, about a Babe in Bethlehem. The Saviour of the world did come, with only a few to welcome.

While shepherds watched their flock by night, an angel spoke in the starlight. "Be not afraid at what I say, for a Child is born unto you this day.

You will find this Babe in a manger, asleep in holy slumber. So go your way and tell, what you did see in Bethlehem."

The Maji came looking for a King, to worship and their gifts to bring. They travelled long coming from afar, guided only by a star.

The star led them unto Bethlehem, where Mary, her Child and Joseph did dwell. The Maji bowed in silent awe when in the house the child they saw.

And in that house, no one did stir, as they opened their treasure. They laid before the Saviour, gold, frankincense, and myrrh.

This Son of David will set us free, and open our eyes that we might see, the glory of the Majesty, in the face of a little Baby.

So, Hallelujah, let us sing, in harmony with the bells that ring. The angel came with good news to tell, God is with us: Immanuel.

No Need To Say Goodbye

(for Andrea)

No more letters, no more sighs, no more tears to fill our eyes. No more going our separate ways, no more long and lonely days.

There's no more dreaming in the night, wishing I could hold you tight. There's not a thing this world can do, to stop my heart from loving you. Loving you, I can't stop - loving you.

Now that we are together, and you are by my side, the way may be long before us, but we've got love, we've got our love - right by our side.

So, no more driving home alone, in the Honda out on my own. There is not a song that can make us cry - why? Cause there's now - no need to say goodbye - to say goodbye - no need to say goodbye.

It’s The Thought That Counts

(for our Mary Rose)

It’s the thought that counts, in everything that we do.

It’s not just what we say, or what we pay for something new.

Silver paper and ribbons of gold, make all things beautiful - that’s what, we were told.

It’s the thought that counts, when we say, "How are you?"

And share the time of day, to help someone along their way.

So let love and kindness, be in all you do, and may the favour of God be always with you - it’s the thought that counts.

We thank you, Mary Rose, for opening our eyes, for helping us to see, and, to realise.

It’s the thought that counts, when everything is said and done.

When all the people will come, to stand before the throne of the Son.

Then the light will shine on every secret part, and the way will be open then into every heart then our thoughts will count.

So, Mary, we want you to know; that you will always be, sweet, Mary Rose.

Our sweet Mary Rose.

Dann zählen unsere gedanken.

The Best Is Yet To Come

(for Marching)

When we started out it was quarter to three, but the time doesn't matter, doesn't matter to me.

Just as long I've got you by my side - as my friend and my guide.

The day is getting longer, it's almost done, and there is a dark cloud moving over the sun.

But we don't care - for the best is yet to come.

We don't look back, no no. No - that's not the way, the way we go.

We don't turn to the left, or to the right, we fix our gaze, on the light.

We keep moving forward, and moving along, though the thunderhead coming, is big and strong.

But we don't care, for the best is yet to come.

The best is yet to come my friend, that's what we believe. There's a promise, in the Book - for everyone to receive.

We see breakthroughs coming on every side. We see the darkness running, running to hide.

And we lift our voice, to the King, for His praise we sing.

For God gave to us, a brand-new heart, it was the plan, from the start. So, we don't care -for the best is yet to come.

ER GAB UNS EIN BRANDNEUES HERZ.

DAS BESTE KOMMT ALSO NOCH.

Training In Winter

(for Tim Muter)

Now the wall is cold to the palms of my hands, as I lean forward and push against it to stretch my calves.

Now the air is cool on my face, as I twist and turn alone on the grass, dancing with my shadow.

Tonight, there is a crescent moon shining in a sky full of stars as I lift my eyes and gaze in awe; at the Father's heavenly lights.

Miro con asombro y asombro.

He Is The One

(with thanks to George Scullion)

The heavens declare the glory of God, the sky is the work of His hands. Day after day, night after night, their voices are heard, are heard to the ends of the world.

He is the one, who made the sky and the sun. He is the one, who made the land and the sea, and for sure, he made you and me.

Now that we know him, come let us praise Him, for the things He has made - all things in heaven, all things on earth, everything came by His grace and His wonderful word.

He is the Lord, our King and our God - He is the Lord, our King and our God. Our Lord, our Saviour, our God.

Jesus is coming, we know that he is coming, for he promised he would. The Lord, He is coming, look up He is coming, lift up your eyes, rejoice, your salvation has come, Jesus-Jesus-our Lord- and our God.

Los ceilos declaren la gloria de Dios.

The Messenger

(for Dot & Alan)

He came with a message in 57, to show New York the way to heaven.

To open blind eyes and help them see - there is a way through the darkness – a way to get free.

A way to get free.

But the city was filled with so many distractions, and the tall cowboys were the main attraction.

And the music was loud on their record machines, and the teenage boys all wore blue jeans - the teenage boys all wore blue jeans.

But who will tell them, if he does not tell them, how will they know the way to go?

They will not read it in a paper or see it at the movies. And who will tell them on the radio? How will they know the way to go?

Now the years had gone by, and he is old and grey, still they came to the park to hear what he would say.

The message went out from those giant screens- now his children's - children all wear blue jeans- his children's, children - they wear blue jeans.

So, if you see a messenger heading your way, be sure that you listen to what he will say.

He can open blind eyes and help us to see, there is a way through the darkness, a way to get free.

Una forma de liberarse.

Life

(for Andrea)

There is life going on all around us, for we belong to a great living cosmos.

Delicate creatures go flittering about and then land - when we are still, they may come to settle on our hand.

He said that 'even when she was young, she would not harm anything that did fly' and when we come to understand, we will know the reason why.

The songbird causes us to lift up our eyes, to see from where such a sweet melody does arise.

We hear the wind and the sound of rustling leaves - all this, for any sense of loneliness to relieve.

Now then, consider! In whose presence do we dwell? Surely, all these things are made so as to tell.

Pueden venir a asentarse en nuestro mano.

Cala D'Or

(by Andrea)

<u>From a balcony in the hotel at Majorca.</u>

Twilight in Majorca - Maxfield Parish blue.

Warm sweet coffee - Warm sweet air.

Peacefulness – Calm.

The dark green line of trees.

Dark green against a background of blue-

studded with foreign stars.

Tranquilidad - Paz y Calma.

About the Author

Alfred was born in the then village of Percy Main which is near to the town of North Shields. Now he is at home in the Marden Estate which is near to Cullercoats on the northeast coast of England.

Alfred has one daughter Andrea, who lives with her husband Steve in Appin on the west coast of Scotland.

Printed in Great Britain
by Amazon

38319592R00046